Contents

T0350575

Welcome

1. ✏️ **Match and trace.**

① ② ③ ④

ⓐ ⓑ ⓒ ⓓ

Hello. I'm
Rita.

Hello. I'm
Zak.

Hello. My name's
Oscar.

Hello. My name's
Millie.

2 **Trace. Then colour.**

| ① | ② | ③ | ④ |

blue   *red*   *yellow*   *green*

3 (1:06) **Listen and tick (✓). Then colour.**

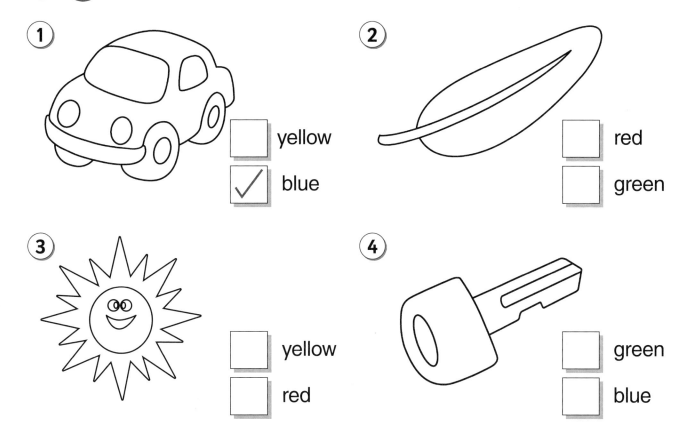

① ☐ yellow
   ✓ blue

② ☐ red
   ☐ green

③ ☐ yellow
   ☐ red

④ ☐ green
   ☐ blue

4 ✏ **Read and trace.**

a 1 _one_
b 2 _two_
c 3 _three_
d 4 _four_
e 5 _five_

f 6 _six_
g 7 _seven_
h 8 _eight_
i 9 _nine_
j 10 _ten_

5 ✏ **Count and trace.**

a _one / two_

b _four / five_

c _eight / nine_

d _six / seven_

e _three / four_

6 Colour in. Then match and trace.

1 **2** **3** **4**

a Her
name's Rita.

b Her
name's Millie.

c His
name's Zak.

d His
name's Oscar.

7 Read and colour.

1 **2**

His backpack is blue.   Her backpack is red.

8 🔘 1:12 **Listen and number. Then write.**

a

b 1

sit down

c

d

e

f

g

h

9 ✏️ **Follow and colour.**

1 2

2 5

3 7

4 9

a red

b yellow

c blue

d green

10 ✏️ **Read and match.**

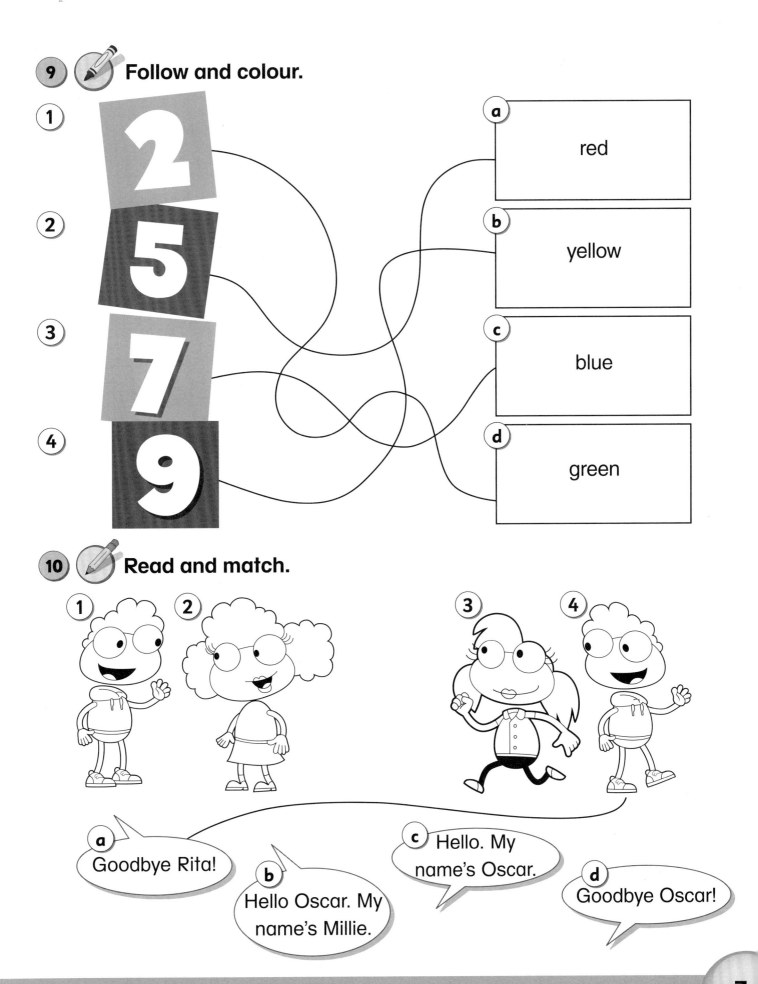

1 2 3 4

a Goodbye Rita!

b Hello Oscar. My name's Millie.

c Hello. My name's Oscar.

d Goodbye Oscar!

1 My birthday

1 Trace and colour.

1 *pink*

2 *orange*

3 *black*

4 *brown*

5 *purple*

6 *white*

Lesson 1 vocabulary (colours)

2 **Listen and number.**

3 **Look and trace. Then colour.**

a I'm ____*four*____ . My favourite colour is *orange*.

b I'm ____*seven*____ . My favourite colour is ____*blue*____ .

c I'm ____*nine*____ . My favourite colour is ____*pink*____ .

d I'm ____*ten*____ . My favourite colour is ____*purple*____ .

Lesson 2 grammar (*What's your name? How old are you? What's your favourite colour?*)

9

4 ✏️ **Match. Then trace.**

1
2
3
4
5
6
7
8

a *stamp*
b *climb*
c *run*
d jump
e *dance*
f *clap*
g *hop*
h *walk*

5   **Read and trace. Then colour.**

1

What colour is it?

It's _purple_.

2

What colour is it?

It's _orange_.

3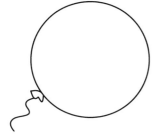

What colour _is it_ ?

It's blue.

4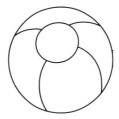

What colour is it?

_It's_ yellow.

5

Is it red?

_No_, it isn't. It's pink.

6

Is it brown?

Yes, it is.

7

Is it white?

No, _it isn't_. It's green.

8

Is it black?

Yes, _it is_.

11

Lesson 4 grammar (*Is it purple? Yes, it is. / No, it isn't. What colour is it? It's blue.*)

6 **Read and circle. Then draw and colour.**

1 Two green cakes for Oscar / Zak.

2 Two purple cakes for Rita / Millie.

3 Two orange cakes for Zak / Millie.

4 Two pink cakes for Oscar / Rita.

5 Eight / ten cakes for Waldo.

7 **Look and write (✓) or (✗) .**

8 ✏️ **Read the words and circle.**

~~pat~~   tap

9 🔊 1:26 **Listen to the sounds and circle the letters.**

1   t ⓟ a s

2   p s t a

3   s t p a

4   t a s p

10 🔊 1:27 **Listen and write the letters.**

1 _t_   2 _____   3 _____   4 _____

11 🔊 1:28 **Listen and write the words.**

1 _s a t_   2 _____   3 _____   4 _____

Lesson 6 phonics (a, p, s, t)

13

12 🖊 **Match. Then trace.**

flower

butterfly

leaf

fish

bird

13 🖍 **Colour. Then circle.**

(fish) (leaf) (bird)   (flower) (butterfly) (bird)

Wider World

14 ✏️ **Trace and match.**

1. *birthday cake*
2. *birthday card*
3. *balloon*
4. *present*

a.
b.
c.
d.

15 ✏️ **Draw and colour. Then write.**

1. How old are you? _____

2. How many balloons? _____

3. What colour is the present? _____

Unit Review

16 **Read and colour.**

1	black
2	brown
3	blue
4	purple
5	pink
6	orange
7	green

17 **Look and circle.**

1 What's your name?   My name's Zak. / Her name's Zak.

2 How old are you?   It's six. / I'm six.

3 What's your favourite colour?   My favourite colour is blue. / His favourite colour is blue.

About Me

18 **Read and write. Then colour.**

pink ~~My~~ is I'm

Hello. ¹_____ My _____ name's Ana.

² _____ seven.

My favourite colour
³ _____ pink.

Look! A ⁴ _____ butterfly!

Goodbye!

19 **Draw and write.**

Hello. My name's

_____.

I'm _____.

My favourite colour is

_____.

Goodbye!

2 At school

1 🖉 Draw. Then trace.

① rubber

② pen

③ pencil

④ pencil sharpener

⑤ pencil case

⑥ ruler

⑦ book

⑧ table

⑨ chair

⑩ desk

Lesson 1 vocabulary (classroom objects)

2 ✏️ **Read and match. Then colour.**

1 It's a pencil sharpener. It's green.

a

2 It's a table. It's brown.

b

3 It's a chair. It's orange.

c

4 It's a rubber. It's red and blue.

d

3 💿 1:38 **Listen, circle and tick (✓).**

1 (black) / blue

☐   ✓

2 pink / brown

☐   ☐

3 purple / green

☐   ☐

4 red / yellow

☐   ☐

Lesson 2 grammar (*What's this? It's a book. It's red. It's a red book.*)

4 🖊 **Match and trace.**

11 **13** **15** **17** **19**

12 **14** **16** **18** **20**

a sixteen

e fourteen

i nineteen

c eleven

g fifteen

b eighteen

d twenty

f thirteen

h seventeen

j twelve

5 🖊 **Read and circle.**

fifteen pencils.

twelve rulers.

6 🔊 1:42 **Listen and number. Then colour.**

a □ **b** 1 **c** □ **d** □

7 ✏️ **Read and circle. Then tick (✓).**

1 What's this? / What are (these?)

It's a chair.
They're chairs. ✓

2 What's this? / What are these?

It's a pen.
They're pens.

3 What's this? / What are these?

It's a table.
They're tables.

4 What's this? / What are these?

It's a pencil sharpener.
They're pencil sharpeners.

21

Lesson 4 grammar (*What are these? They're pencils. What colour are they? They're red.*)

8 🎧 1:43 **Listen and tick (✓).**

	1	2	3	4	5
Yes	✓	☐	☐	☐	☐
No	☐	☐	☐	☐	☐

9 ✏️ **Read and trace.**

This is my ~~mum~~ .

10 ✏️ **Write (✓) or (✗) for what you do at school.**

11 ✏️ **Read the words and circle.**

dip   man   nap   pan

12 🎧 1:48 **Listen to the sounds and circle the letters.**

1
a d
m n

2
d m
i
p

3
i
a
n t

4
p
d
i
t

13 🎧 1:49 **Listen and write the letters.**

1 _m_   2 _____   3 _____   4 _____

14 🎧 1:50 **Listen and write the words.**

1 _s i t_   2 _____   3 _____   4 _____

15 Match and trace.

piano   guitar   drum   violin

16 Read and circle.

It's a (guitar / drum).

It's a (piano / violin).

It's a (piano / drum).

Wider World

17 Trace and match.

1. school
2. playground
3. classroom
4. teacher
5. pupil

a
b
c
d
e

18 Look at your classroom. Count and write.

1. How many tables can you see? I can see seven tables.

2. How many chairs can you see? _____

3. How many books can you see? _____

4. How many backpacks can you see? _____

5. How many pencil cases can you see? _____

6. What colour is your pencil case? _____

Unit Review

19 **Read and match. Then colour.**

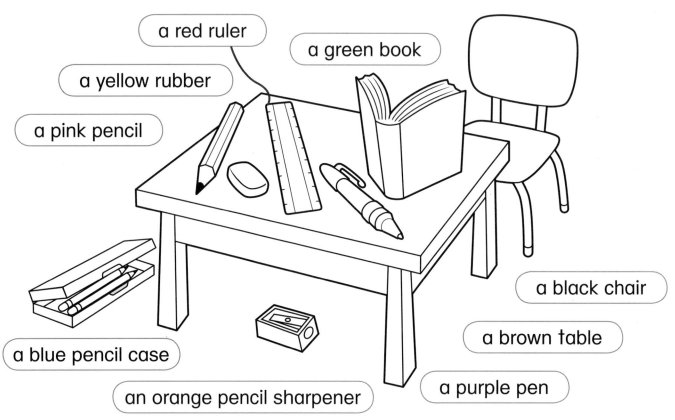

a red ruler

a green book

a yellow rubber

a pink pencil

a black chair

a brown table

a blue pencil case

an orange pencil sharpener

a purple pen

20 **Join the dots. Then read and circle.**

1

2

What's this? / What are these?

It's a book. / They're pencils.

What's this? / What are these?

It's a backpack. / They're rulers.

About Me

21 Read and circle. Then colour.

1 ((This) / These) is my desk.

2 (This / These) are my books.

They're red and blue.

And 3 (this / these) is my pencil case. It's pink.

Can you see two pens?

They're green.

22 Draw your desk and write.

This is my _____.

These are my _____.
They're _____.

And this is my _____.
It's _____.

Can you see _____?
They're _____.

3 My family

1 **Trace and number.**

1 dad 2 mum 3 sister 4 brother

This is my family.

5 grandad

6 granny

7 friend

Read and circle. Then find and colour.

This is my (mum / (friend)).

He's ((nine) / ten).

This is my (granny / sister).

She's (seven / eight).

 Trace and match.

| seven | five | ~~eight~~ | ten |

1 How old is he? He's _eight_.

2 How old is she? She's _seven_.

3 How old is she? She's _five_.

4 How old is he? He's _ten_.

Lesson 2 grammar (*This is my brother/sister. How old is he/she? He's/She's nine.*)

29

4 **Look and write.**

vet   pilot   doctor   dentist   ~~cook~~   artist   farmer   dancer

a

cook

b

_____

c

_____

d

_____

e

_____

f

_____

g

_____

h

_____

5 **Read and circle.**

My mum / dad
is a farmer / doctor.

My mum / dad
is a pilot / teacher.

6 ✏️ **Match. Then read and circle.**

1 Is she a doctor? (Yes, she is.) / No, she isn't.

2 Is she an artist? Yes, she is. / No, she isn't.

3 Is he a vet? Yes, he is. / No, he isn't.

4 Is he a teacher? Yes, he is. / No, he isn't.

7 🔊 1:64 **Listen and tick (✓). Then write.**

| ~~cook~~ doctor artist pilot |

1
☐ Yes, he is.
✓ No, he isn't.
He's a ___cook___.

2
☐ Yes, she is.
☐ No, she isn't.
She's a _____.

3
☐ Yes, he is.
☐ No, he isn't.
He's an _____.

4
☐ Yes, she is.
☐ No, she isn't.
She's a _____.

31

Lesson 4 grammar (*Is he/she a vet? Yes, he/she is. No he/she isn't. He's/She's a Cook.*)

8 Read and find. Then circle.

1 This is my mum. She's a pilot. a b

2 This is my friend. His name's Waldo. a b

3 This is my brother. He's six. a b

9 Match and trace. Then colour.

1 dad
2 mum
3 granny
4 grandad
5 sister
6 brother
me

10 🖊 **Read the words and circle.**

~~can~~ cap dig dog

11 🎧 (1:69) **Listen to the sounds and circle the letters.**

1
g   c
⊙   t

2
c   o
g   a

3
g
i   p
a

4
o   a
c   g

12 🎧 (1:70) **Listen and write the letters.**

1 _c_   2 _____   3 _____

13 🎧 (1:71) **Listen and write the words.**

1 _g a s_   2 _____   3 _____   4 _____

14 Read and write.

drawing   sculpture   ~~painting~~   collage

1 It's a _painting_.

a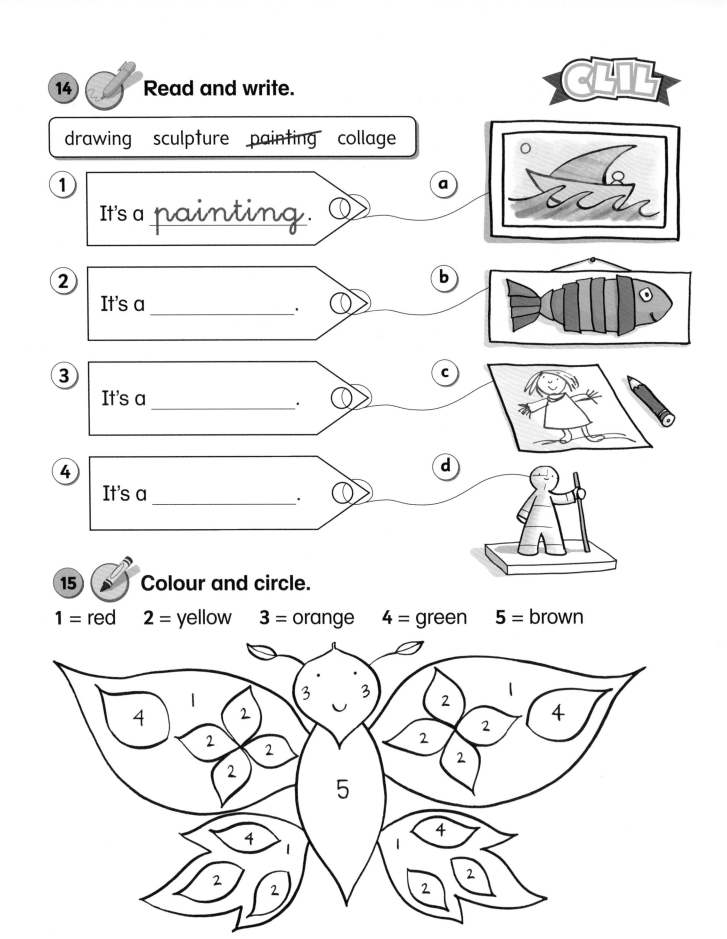

2 It's a _____.

b

3 It's a _____.

c

4 It's a _____.

d

15 Colour and circle.

1 = red   **2** = yellow   **3** = orange   **4** = green   **5** = brown

It's a painting / collage. It's a bird / butterfly.

Wider World

16 **Look and draw. Then listen and number.**

17 **Read and answer. Then ask a friend.**

Yes, he is.   No, he isn't.   Yes, she is.   No, she isn't.

	me	my friend
Is your dad a farmer?		
Is your mum an artist?		
Is your brother a cook?		
Is your sister a dancer?		

Unit Review

18 1:77 **Listen. Circle *True* or *False*.**

This is my *family*.

1 (True.) / False.
2 True. / False.
3 True. / False.
4 True. / False.
5 True. / False.

19 **Look at Activity 18. Read and circle.**

1 This is my (mum) / dad. She's a vet / (pilot.)

2 This is my dad / grandad. He's a doctor / dentist.

3 This is my sister / brother. His / Her name's Rita.

4 This is my sister / brother. His / Her name's Vava.

5 This is Oscar / Millie. He's / She's my friend.

About Me

20 **Read and write.**

mum	~~dad~~	brother

This is my family. This is my
¹ _dad_ . He's a doctor.
His name's Paul.

My ² _____ is a vet.
Her name's Alice.

And this is my ³ _____ .
He's two! His name's Sam.

21 **Draw one person in your family and write.**

This is my _____ .

He's / She's a _____ .

His / Her name's _____
.

4 My body

1 Look and write. Then colour.

| head | toes | feet | legs | hands | body | fingers | arms |

1 *head*

2 _____

3 _____

4 _____

5 _____

6 _____

7 _____

8 _____

2 **Read. Then circle.**

	a	**b**	**c**
1 feet			
2 wings			
3 tail			
4 arms			

3 (2:06) **Listen and circle. Then colour.**

1 I've got a (pink / purple) body.

2 I've got (brown / orange) hands.

3 I've got (yellow / blue) feet.

4 **Read and match. Then write and colour.**

| socks | skirt | T-shirt | hat | dress | jumper | trousers | ~~shoes~~ |

1 I've got brown shoes.   **a** _____

2 I've got a pink hat.   **b** _____

3 I've got a red dress.   **c** _____

4 I've got purple socks.   **d** *shoes*

5 I've got a green jumper.   **e** _____

6 I've got black trousers.   **f** _____

7 I've got a blue skirt.   **g** _____

8 I've got a grey T-shirt.   **h** _____

5 **Count and write. Then colour.**

six four eight ~~one~~

1 She's got *one* head. It's red.

2 She's got _____ arms. They're black.

3 She's got _____ feet. They're blue.

4 She's got _____ toes. They're yellow.

5 She's got a green dress.

  6 **Follow. Then choose and write.**

 1

2

3

4

 a

 b

 c

d

1 (He's)/ She's got a <u>*hat*</u> .

2 He's / She's got a _____ .

3 He's / She's got _____ .

4 He's / She's got _____ .

Lesson 4 grammar (*He's got blue trousers./She's got a yellow head.*)

7 **Listen and colour. Then write.**

pink   blue   ~~yellow~~   red

1   **2**   **3**

Millie has got _yellow_ hands.

Zak has got _____ feet.

Vava has got _____ feet and a _____ body.

8 **Look and tick (✓).**

Lesson 5 story and values (be clean)

9 ✏️ **Read the words and circle.**

kick   kid   neck   sock

ck   e   k

10 💿 2:15 **Listen to the sounds and circle the letters.**

1
k
e   (i)
a

2
d
t   k
e

3
a
e   k
o

4
a
i   ck
g

11 💿 2:16 **Listen and write the letters.**

1 _k_   2 _____   3 _____

12 💿 2:17 **Listen and write the words.**

1 _k i t_   2 _____   3 _____   4 _____

14 **Listen and check your answers.**

Wider World

15 🖉 **Carnival masks. Read and match.**

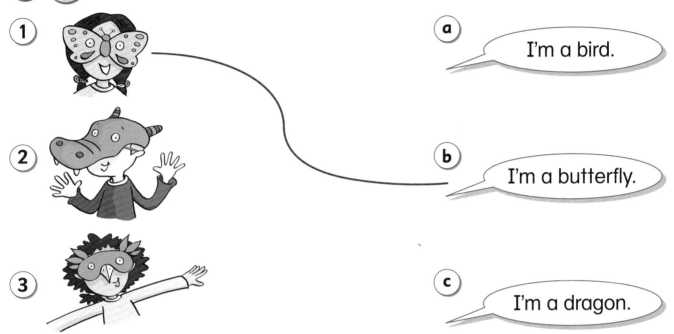

16 🖌 **Choose a carnival costume. Colour and write.**

This is my carnival costume.

I've got _____ and a _____.

Unit Review

17 **Read and circle. Then colour.**

1   I've got a (body / (foot)).

((It's) / They're) green.

a

2   I've got three (finger / fingers).

(It's / They're) pink.

b

3   I've got five (leg / legs).

(It's / They're) brown.

c

4   I've got (feet / foot).

(It's / They're) orange.

d

18 **Look and write (✓) or (✗).**

1   He's got a clean T-shirt.

2   She's got a dirty dress.

3   He's got dirty boots.

4   She's got clean shoes.

About Me

19 **Read and write. Then colour.**

arms   eight   ~~head~~   three

This is my monster. He's got one ¹ _head_ . It's yellow. He's got a green body.

He's got two ² _____. They're pink. And he's got ³ _____ purple fingers.

He's got three legs. They're blue. And he's got ⁴ _____ black feet.

He's got a green hat. His name's Spike!

20 **Draw a monster and write.**

This is my monster.

He's got one _____.

It's _____.

He's got _____.

They're _____.

He's got_____.

They're _____.

His name's _____!

5 Pets

1 **Look and write.**

frog   cat   dog   hamster   mouse   ~~parrot~~   rabbit   snake   tortoise

1

parrot

2

_____

3

_____

4

_____

5

_____

6

_____

7

_____

8

_____

9

_____

Find and circle.

1 a snake **2** two frogs **3** a parrot **4** a tortoise **5** three mice

 Look at Activity 2. Read and circle.

1 (What's that?) / What are those? (It's a snake.) / They're snakes.

2 What's that? / What are those? It's a frog. / They're frogs.

3 What's that? / What are those? It's a parrot. / They're parrots.

4 What's that? / What are those? It's a tortoise. / They're tortoises.

5 What's that? / What are those? It's a mouse. / They're mice.

Lesson 2 grammar (*What's that? It's a dog. What are those? They're rabbits.*)

4 **Look and write.**

| big | ~~small~~ | tall | short | thin | fat | young | old |

1. *small*
2.
3.
4.

5.
6.
7.
8.

5 **Look and write.**

| frog | ~~rabbit~~ | cat | dog |

1 He's got a *rabbit* .   3 He's got a _____ .

2 She's got a _____ .   4 She's got a _____ .

6 **Listen, look and tick (✓).**

1 Yes, he has. ✓

No, he hasn't.

2 Yes, she has.

No, she hasn't.

3 Yes, he has.

No, he hasn't.

4 Yes, she has.

No, she hasn't.

5 Yes, he has.

No, he hasn't.

6 Yes, she has.

No, she hasn't.

7 **Read and circle about your pets.**

1 Have you got a big dog? Yes, I have. / No, I haven't.

2 Have you got a small dog? Yes, I have. / No, I haven't.

3 Have you got a fat cat? Yes, I have. / No, I haven't.

4 Have you got a small rabbit? Yes, I have. / No, I haven't.

5 Have you got an old cat? Yes, I have. / No, I haven't.

51

Lesson 4 grammar (*Have you got a parrot? Yes, I have. / No, I haven't.*)

8 **Look and number.**

 9 **Read and circle.**

Waldo is a (dragon) / tortoise. He's got two / three arms and two / three legs. He has / hasn't got wings. He's young / old.

10 **Who lives here? Look, match and say.**

11 ✏️ **Read the words and circle.**

bag   cup   hat   rat

12 (2:38) **Listen to the sounds and circle the letters.**

1   r
     n   b
       (h)

2   h
       u
     r
       b

3   b
     a
        r
     u

4   n
        h
     b
        p

13 (2:39) **Listen and write the letters.**

1 _r_   2 ____   3 ____   4 ____

14 (2:40) **Listen and write the words.**

1 _u p_   2 ____   3 ____   4 ____

15 **Write. Then match.**

chick   kitten   puppy

1 _____

2 _____

3 _____

16 **Join the dots. Then read and circle.**

It's a (kitten / puppy / chick).   It's a (kitten / puppy / chick).

Wider World

17 Follow and write.

rat   tortoise   snake   ~~spider~~

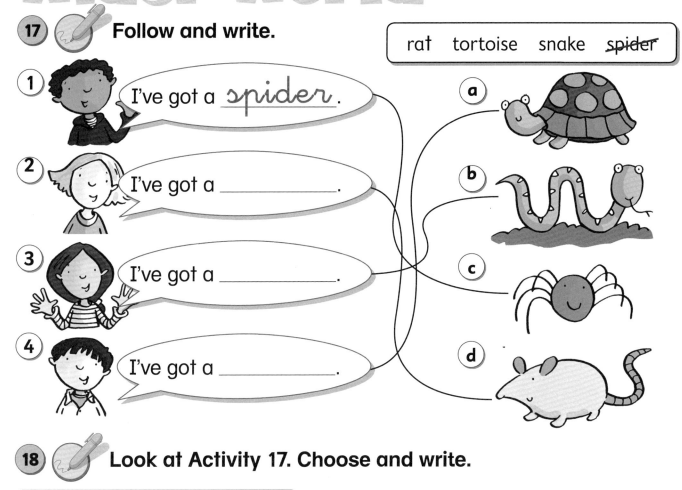

1 I've got a _spider_.

2 I've got a _____.

3 I've got a _____.

4 I've got a _____.

a

b

c

d

18 Look at Activity 17. Choose and write.

Yes, I have.   No, I haven't.

Have you got a snake?

1 _____.

Have you got a snake?

2 _____.

19 Read and answer.

1 Have you got an unusual pet? _____

2 What pet have you got? _____

Unit Review

  Read and answer.

Yes, he has. No, he hasn't. Yes, she has. No, she hasn't.

1

1 Has he got a dog?

Yes, he has .

2 Has she got a rabbit?

_____

2

3 Has he got a parrot?

_____

4 Has she got a frog?

_____

21 **Read and match. Then write.**

thin   small   ~~old~~   long   young   ~~fat~~

1 What's that?

It's a dog. It's __old__ and __fat__ .

2 What are those?

They're snakes. They're _____ and _____.

3 What are those?

They're kittens. They're _____ and _____.

a

b

c

About Me

22 **Read and circle. Then colour.**

I've got a ¹ (puppy / (kitten)).

He's ² (black / blue) and white.

He's got ³ (two / four) legs.

He's got a ⁴ (long / short) tail.

⁵ (His / Her) name's Minty.

23 **Draw a pet and write.**

I've got a _____.

He's / She's _____ and

_____.

He's / She's got _____ legs.

He's / She's got a _____ tail.

His / Her name's _____.

6 My house

1 ✏️ **Draw then write.**

bathroom   bedroom   garden   door   kitchen
living room   ~~window~~

1 window

Lesson 1 vocabulary (rooms in the house)

2 2:51 **Listen and number. Then read and match.**

He's in the bathroom.

She's in the bedroom.

She's in the kitchen.

They're in the living room.

3 **Join the dots. Then read and circle.**

(Where's / Where are) Waldo?

He's in the (kitchen / living room).

Lesson 2 grammar (*Where's my dad/mum? He's/She's in the living room.*)

59

4 2:54 **Listen and number.**

a □

b 1

c □

d □

e □

f □

g □

h □

5 **Look, read, and circle.**

1 They're in the
(bathroom / bedroom).

2 They're in the
(living room / bathroom).

3 They're in the
(garden / kitchen).

6 **Read and find. Then circle and write.**

| bed | desk | fridge | sofa | ~~table~~ | bath |

1 Where is the lamp?

The lamp ((is) / are) on the ___*table*___ .

2 Where are the rabbits?

The rabbits are (on / in) the _____ .

3 Where is the teddy bear?

It is (under / in) the _____ .

4 Where is the boy?

He is (on / in) the _____ .

5 Where are the books?

The books (is / are) on the _____ .

6 Where are the dogs?

The dogs are (on / under) the _____ .

Lesson 4 grammar (*There's a lamp on the desk. There are two kittens on the sofa.*)

7 ✏️ **Look and match. Then write.**

| bathroom kitchen ~~living room~~ bedroom |

Dad is in the _living room_. Zak is in the _____.

Rita is in her _____. Vava and Waldo are in the _____.

8 ✏️ **Look and draw.**

My bedroom

9 ✏️ **Read the words and circle.**

~~bell~~   doll   fan   leg

10 (2:61) **Listen to the sounds and circle the letters.**

1
f
(s)
ff   ll

2
o
h   ff
ll

3
l   h
f   r

4
i   f
t   l

11 (2:62) **Listen and write the letters.**

1 _ll_   2 _____   3 _____   4 _____

12 (2:63) **Listen and write the words.**

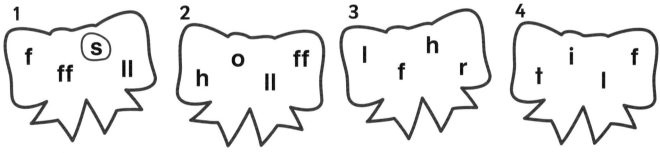

1 _fig_   2 _____   3 _____   4 _____

13 (2:66) **Write. Then listen and follow the path.**

| café | ~~house~~ | library | playground | shop |

1 *house*

2 _____

3 _____

4 _____

5 _____

14 **Find and circle.**

1

She's in the
(zoo / café).

2

It's in the
(shop / park).

3

He's in the
(library / café).

Wider World

15 Read and match.

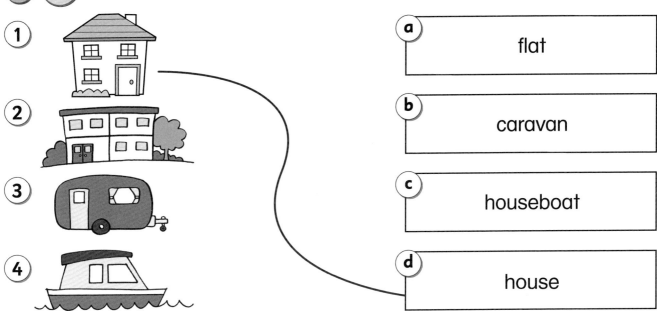

1
2
3
4

a. flat

b. caravan

c. houseboat

d. house

16 Read and complete the letter.

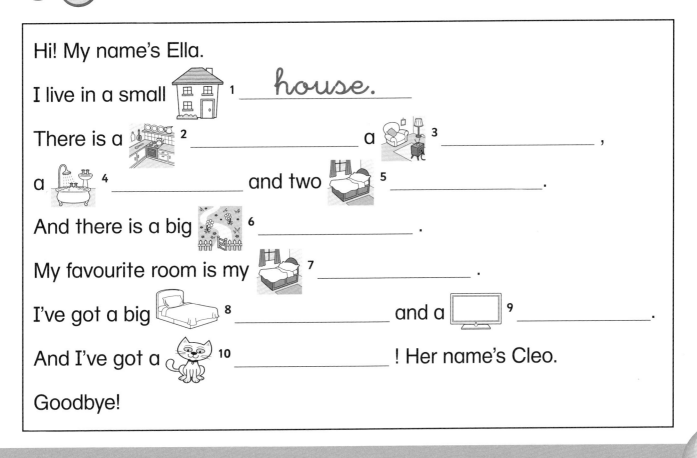

Hi! My name's Ella.

I live in a small 1 _house._

There is a 2 _____ a 3 _____ ,

a 4 _____ and two 5 _____ .

And there is a big 6 _____ .

My favourite room is my 7 _____ .

I've got a big 8 _____ and a 9 _____ .

And I've got a 10 _____ ! Her name's Cleo.

Goodbye!

Unit Review

2:69 **Listen and draw.**

About Me

18 **Read and write.**

lamp   ~~bedroom~~   chairs   big   two

My favourite room is my

1 _bedroom_ .

It's 2 _____ .

There are 3 _____

beds and two 4 _____ .

There's a table.

There's a 5 _____ on

the table.

I've got a TV.

19 **Draw your favourite room and write.**

My favourite room is my

_____ .

It's _____ .

There is _____ .

There are _____ .

I've got a _____ .

7 Food

1 🖊️ **Draw. Then write.**

bread	cheese	chicken	fruit	juice
~~meat~~	milk	lemonade	salad	yoghurt

1

meat

2

3

4

5

6

7

8

9

10

2 **Find and colour. Then write (✓) or (✗).**

juice ☐
meat ☐
yoghurt ☐
cheese ☐
fruit ☐
bread ☐
milk ☐
salad ☐
lemonade ☐

I like …

3 **Read and draw.**

I want meat, salad and cheese.

I want juice.

Lesson 2 grammar (*I like salad and meat. What do you want? I want milk.*)

4 🖍️ **Look and number.**

honey ☐   ice cream ☐   water 1   vegetables ☐

jelly ☐   chocolate ☐   sandwich ☐   cake ☐

5 🔈 3:08 **Listen and number. Then circle and write.**

a   b   c   d

☐   ☐   ☐   1

1 I ((like) / don't like) _honey_ .

2 I (like / don't like) _____ .

3 I (like / don't like) _____ .

4 I (like / don't like) _____ .

cheese
(honey)
jelly
meat

6 3:11 **Listen and number.**

a ☐

b ☐

c ☐

d 1

7 **Look and write.**

1

Do you like jelly?

_____, I _____.

2

Do you like honey?

_____, I _____.

Lesson 4 grammar *(Do you like honey? Yes, I do./No, I don't.)*

8 Read and match.

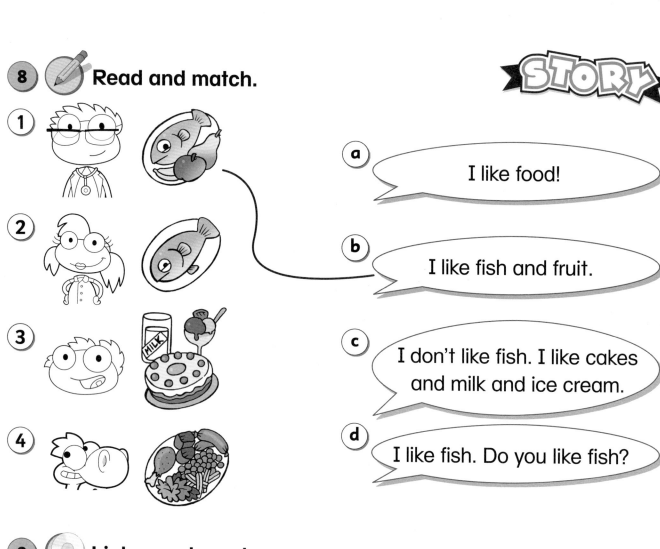

1

2

3

4

a I like food!

b I like fish and fruit.

c I don't like fish. I like cakes and milk and ice cream.

d I like fish. Do you like fish?

STORY

9 3:13 Listen and number.

a

b 1

c

d

10 ✏️ **Read the words and circle.**

jet   kiss   van   wig

11 (3:17) **Listen to the sounds and circle the letters.**

1   ss   v   c   f

2   w   o   u   v

3   j   v   i   w

4   ss   i   v   j

12 (3:18) **Listen and write the letters.**

1   w   2   3   4

13 (3:19) **Listen and write the words.**

1   mess   2   3   4

14 Follow and write.

1

sausages   chips   carrots

a _____

2

b _____

3

c _____

15 Read and tick (✓). Then draw.

It's good for me!

fruit ☐

salad ☐

cake ☐

bread ☐

yoghurt ☐

milk ☐

juice ☐

chocolate ☐

Wider World

16 (3:21) **What does Ella want? Listen and tick (✓).**

Chicken	✓	Rice	☐
Meat	☐	Vegetables	☐
Fish	☐	Salad	☐
Fruit	☐	Water	☐
Ice cream	☐	Juice	☐
Yoghurt	☐	Milk	☐

17 **What do you want? Ask a friend and tick (✓).**

Chicken	☐	Rice	☐
Meat	☐	Vegetables	☐
Fish	☐	Salad	☐
Fruit	☐	Water	☐
Ice cream	☐	Juice	☐
Yoghurt	☐	Milk	☐

Unit Review

18 〔3:25〕 **Listen, draw and match.**

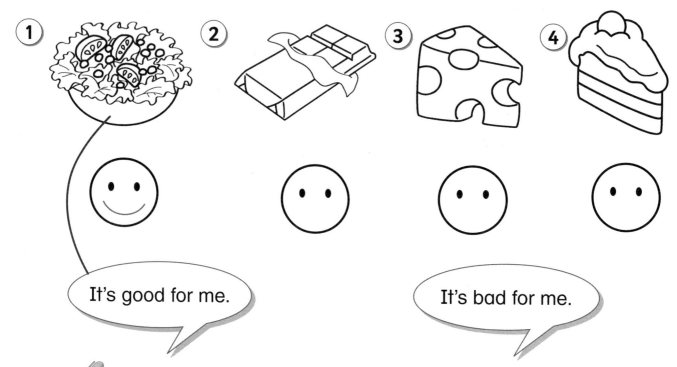

It's good for me.

It's bad for me.

19 🖉 **Read. Then choose and write.**

Yes, I do.   No, I don't.

1 Do you like milk?   Yes, I do.

2 Do you like juice?   _____.

3 Do you like meat?   _____.

About Me

20 **Read and circle.**

I ¹ (like / don't like) chicken and chips.

I ² (like / don't like) fruit.

My favourite food is ³ (pizza / salad).

I ⁴ (like / don't like) sausages.

21 **Draw your favourite food and write.**

I like _____ and

_____ .

I don't like _____ .

My favourite food is

_____ .

8 I'm excited!

1 3:29 **Listen and number. Then write.**

| excited | hungry | scared | ~~thirsty~~ | tired |

a

She's _____.

b

He's _____.

c

She's _*thirsty*_ . **1**

d

He's _____.

e

He's _____.

2 🔊 3:32 **Listen and circle.**

1

Yes, I am.
No, I'm not.

2

Yes, I am.
No, I'm not.

3

Yes, I am.
No, I'm not.

4

Yes, I am.
No, I'm not.

3 ✏️ **Find. Then read and circle.**

1 (He's / She's) (excited / tired).

2 (He's / She's) (thirsty / tired).

3 (He's / She's) (excited / thirsty).

4 (He's / She's) (scared / hungry).

5 (He's / She's) (excited / hungry).

79

Lesson 2 grammar (*I'm/He's/She's excited. Are you hungry? Yes, I am./No, I'm not.*)

Look and write.

| angry | bored | cold | ~~happy~~ | hot | hurt | sad | ill |

1

She's *happy* .

2

He's _____ .

3

He's _____ .

4

She's _____ .

5

She's _____ .

6

He's _____ .

7

She's _____ .

8

He's _____ .

 Read and answer the questions. Then draw yourself.

| Yes, I am.   No, I'm not. |

1   Are you happy? _____

2   Are you cold? _____

3   Are you angry? _____

4   Are you excited? _____

5   Are you hungry? _____

6 🔊 3:36 **Listen and number.**

a

b

c

d

7 ✏️ **Look. Then circle and write.**

1

Are you happy?

Yes, I am. / No, I'm not.

I'm _____.

2

Are they hot?

Yes, they are. / No, they aren't.

They're _____.

3

Is she bored?

Yes, she is. / No, she isn't.

She's _____.

4

Is he tired?

Yes, he is. / No, he isn't.

He's _____.

Lesson 4 grammar (*Is he/she cold? Yes, he/she is. Are they bored? No, they aren't.*)

8 Read and circle.

a He's hot / excited / sad.

b He's hungry / thirsty / ill.

c He's tired / scared / angry.

d He's cold / hot / hungry.

e He's happy / excited / scared.

f He's scared / ill / hurt.

g They're happy / hurt / bored.

9 Look and write.

1

2

3

Are you _____sad_____? Are you _____? Can I _____ you?

10 ✏️ **Read the words and circle.**

box   buzz   taxi   yes

Yes!

TAXI

11 🔊 3:41 **Listen to the sounds and circle the letters.**

1   z   y   j   ⓧ

2   x   z   y   zz

3   ck   qu   zz   y

4   w   x   qu   ck

12 🔊 3:42 **Listen and write the letters.**

1 _z_   2 ____   3 ____   4 ____   5 ____

13 🔊 3:43 **Listen and write the words.**

1 _quiz_   2 _____   3 ____   4 _____

14 **Look and match.**

①

It's a long shadow.

②

③ It's a short shadow.

④

15 **Read, circle and write.**

①

Is it a desk?

Yes, it is. / (No, it isn't).

It's a _chair_ .

②

Is it a hand?

Yes, it is. / No, it isn't.

It's a _____ .

③

Is it a frog?

Yes, it is. / No, it isn't.

It's a _____ .

④

Is it a window?

Yes, it is. / No, it isn't.

It's a _____ .

Wider World

16 (3:45) **A puppet show! Listen, read and write.**

excited ~~dragon~~ presents friends cake birthday

1

Hello. My name's Firefly. I'm a _dragon_.

2

I'm _____ today. It's my birthday.

3

This is my birthday _____. I'm hungry!

4

These are my _____.

5

And these are my _____.

6

Happy _____, Firefly!

Thank you!

Unit Review

17 🔘 3:48 **Listen and number. Then write.**

1 She's _scared_ .

2 She's _____ .

3 He's _____ .

4 They're _____ .

5 He's _____ .

18 ✏️ **Look at Activity 17. Read and circle.**

1 Is Millie scared? (Yes, she is. / No, she isn't.)

2 Is Rita sad? (Yes, she is. / No, she isn't.)

3 Is Zak tired? (Yes, he is. / No, he isn't.)

4 Are Waldo and Vava thirsty? (Yes, they are. / No, they aren't.)

5 Is Oscar thirsty? (Yes, he is. / No, he isn't.)

About Me

19 **Read and circle. Then colour.**

This is me on my birthday. I'm

[1] (happy / sad) and [2] (bored / excited).

I've got [3] (three / five balloons).

They are red, white and blue.

And I'm [4] (hungry / thirsty). I've got

a [5] (big / small) chocolate cake!

20 **Draw yourself on your birthday and write.**

This is me on my _____.

I'm _____ and

_____.

I've got _____ balloons.

They're _____.

I'm _____.

I've got a _____

birthday cake!

Goodbye

 1 **Look and write.**

| bed | blanket | book | egg | torch | ~~milk~~ | mouse | photo | soap |

 1

milk _____

2

_____

3

_____

4

_____

5

_____

6

_____

 7

_____

8

_____

9

_____

2 🖊 **Look, circle and write.**

1 Is it a cat?

((Yes) / No), _it is_ .

2 Is it a pencil?

(Yes / No), _____ .

3 Is it an egg?

(Yes / No), _____ .

4 Is it a backpack?

(Yes / No), _____ .

5 Is it a blanket?

(Yes / No), _____ .

6 Is it a torch?

(Yes / No), _____ .

a

b

c

d

e

f

89

3 🔘 3:53 **Listen and number.**

a b c

d e f `1`

g h i

4 ✏️ **Look and write.**

1 I've got a _____.

2 I've got two _____.

3 _____.

4 _____.

5 ✏️ **Find and circle the odd words out. Then write.**

1 cheese (ruler) meat salad   _ruler_

2 pencil book cat rubber   _____

3 mum dad dancer sister   _____

4 dog shoes rabbit mouse   _____

5 artist brother farmer teacher   _____

6 yoghurt trousers T-shirt hat   _____

7 living room kitchen shop bedroom   _____

8 park bathroom library café   _____

6 ✏️ **Read and answer.**

1 What's your favourite colour? _____

2 What's your favourite animal? _____

3 What's your favourite food? _____

4 Who's your favourite character? _____

Halloween

1 ✏️ Match. Then write.

cat pumpkin bat witch ~~monster~~

1 2 3 4 5

a b c d e

_____   *monster*   _____

2 ✏️ Join the dots. Then circle.

I'm a monster / pumpkin / witch.

Christmas

1 (3:59) **Trace and match. Then listen and colour.**

a sleigh **b** present **c** reindeer **d** Santa

2 **Draw and say. Then read and trace.**

To, _____

Happy Christmas!

From Santa.

Easter

1 **Colour and write.**

| chick egg ~~bunny~~ |

 bunny _____ _____

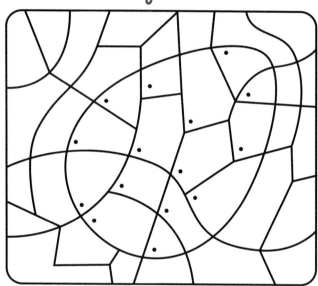

It's an _____.

2 **Look and draw.**

①

②

③

Summer fun

1 **Read and match.**

a sun

b sky

c tree

d bird

e flower

f grass

2 **Choose and write. Then colour the picture in Activity 1.**

blue   brown   purple   yellow   green

The sky is ____blue____. The sun is _____.

The tree is_____. The bird is _____.

The flowers are _____. The grass is _____.

1 Review

1 *Choose and write.*

My   Yes   ~~Hello~~   I'm   it   Her   you   your   is

a ___Hello___. What's your name?

_____ name's Ellie.

b _____ name's Grace.

c How old are _____?

_____ four.

d What's _____ favourite colour?

My favourite colour _____ blue.

e What colour is your backpack? Is _____ blue?

_____, it is.

1 **Choose and write.**

| it | these | ~~this~~ | blue | pencils | They're | many | they | book | Three |

a What's _____ *this* ?

It's a _____.

b Is _____ red?

No, it isn't. It's blue. It's a _____ book.

c What are _____ ?

They're _____.

d What colour are _____ ?

_____ purple.

e How _____ pencils can you see?

_____.

3

1 **Choose and write.**

this   Is   ~~He's~~   She's   my   No   she

a
This is my brother.
__He's__ ten.

How old is
_____ ?

b
And _____ is
my sister.

c
_____ five.

d
This is
_____ mum.

_____ she
a dentist?

e
_____ , she
isn't. She's a vet.

1 **Choose and write.**

He's   I've   ~~got~~   They're

a

He's ___got___ a blue head and a red body.

b

_____ got four arms. They're green.

c

He's got three legs. _____ blue.

d

_____ got a red head and a green body. I've got blue feet.

5

1 ✏️ **Choose and write.**

| are | It's | They're | long | you | Has | ~~What's~~ | hasn't | I've |

a What's that?

_____ a big cat.

b What _____ those?

_____ rats.

c _____ she got a rat?

No, she _____ . She's got a hamster.

d Have _____ got a rat?

No, I haven't. _____ got a snake.

It's a _____ snake!

1   **Choose and write.**

are Where's under There's She's They're ~~Where~~

a

Where are Mum and Dad?

_____ in the living room.

b

Where's Grace?

_____ in the bedroom.

c

Hmm. _____ a lamp on the desk. There _____ two rabbits on the bed.

_____ Grace?

d

She's _____ the bed.

1 **Choose and write.**

| please | Yes | Thank | ~~like~~ | don't | want | Do | What |

a

I __*like*__ sandwiches and fruit. I _____ like chicken.

b

_____ you like chicken, Grace?

_____ , I do. I like chicken. I don't like sandwiches!

c

_____ do you want?

I _____ chicken. What do you want?

d

I want sandwiches, _____ .

Here you are.

e

_____ you!

1 **Choose and write.**

Are   you   they   ~~I'm~~   am   He's   he

a

I'm thirsty.

And ___I'm___ hungry.

b

Are _____ hungry?

Yes, I _____.

c

Is _____ hungry?

No, he isn't. _____ thirsty.

d

Here you are.

Thank you.

e

_____ they happy?

Yes, _____ are.

Picture dictionary

Unit 1

 My birthday

| red | yellow | green | blue | pink | purple | orange | brown | black | white |

 Numbers (1)

| one | two | three | four | five | six | seven | eight | nine | ten |

 Actions

| jump | walk | stamp | clap | run | dance | climb | hop |

 CLIL: Science

| bird | fish | flower | leaf | butterfly |

Unit 2

Stick Classroom objects

chair   table   pencil   ruler   pen

rubber   book   desk   pencil sharpener   pencil case

 ## Numbers (2)

eleven   twelve   thirteen   fourteen   fifteen

sixteen   seventeen   eighteen   nineteen   twenty

 ## CLIL: Music

guitar   piano   violin   drum

Unit 3

 My family

mum   dad   brother   sister   friend   granny   grandad

 Occupations

doctor   cook   vet   dentist

pilot   artist   dancer   farmer

 CLIL: Art

painting   collage   drawing   sculpture

Unit 4

 My body

head

arms

feet

hands

body

fingers

legs

toes

wings

tail

 Clothes

T-shirt

jumper

trousers

dress

skirt

shoes

socks

hat

 CLIL: Science

clean hands

dirty hands

a dirty face

wash your hands

Unit 5

 Pets

dog

cat

rabbit

parrot

mouse

tortoise

frog

snake

hamster

 Opposites

big

small

tall

short

long

thin

fat

young

old

 CLIL: Science

chick

kitten

puppy

egg

goose

bird

Unit 6

 My house (1)

kitchen

living room

door

garden

bathroom

bedroom

window

house

 My house (2)

bath

cooker

fridge

TV

sofa

lamp

bed

sink

 CLIL: Social Science

shop

library

playground

café

zoo

park

Unit 7

Stick Food (1)

meat	fruit	bread	cheese	yoghurt
milk	juice	chicken	salad	lemonade

Food (2)

sandwich   water   chocolate   honey

jelly   vegetables   ice cream   cake

CLIL: Social Science

sausages   chips   carrots

Unit 8

 Feelings (1)

happy   sad   excited   scared   tired   hungry   thirsty

 Feelings (2)

hot   cold   ill   hurt   angry   bored

 CLIL: Science

a long shadow

a short shadow

Pearson Education Limited
Edinburgh Gate
Harlow
Essex CM20 2JE
England
and Associated Companies throughout the world.

www.islands.pearson.com

© Pearson Education Limited 2012

First published 2012
Seventh impression 2018
ISBN: 978-1-4479-0310-9

Set in Fiendstar 17/21pt
Printed in Slovakia by Neografia

Picture Credits
The Publisher would like to thank the following for their kind permission to reproduce their photographs:

(Key: b-bottom; c-centre; l-left; r-right; t-top)

Stickers Page Fotolia.com: Viktor (chicken); Pics721 (house); Matka Wariatka (pencil case); Jose Manuel Gelpi (pencil sharpener); Coprid (desk); Artemisphoto (salad); Anna Kucherova (lemonade). **Shutterstock.com:** V. J. Matthew (garden). **105 Fotolia.com:** Matka_Wariatka (pencil case); Jose Manuel Gelpi (pencil sharpener); Coprid (desk). **109 Fotolia.com:** Pics721 (house). **Shutterstock.com:** V. J. Matthew (garden). **111 Fotolia.com:** Viktor (chicken); Artemisphoto (salad); Anna Kucherova (lemonade)

All other images © Pearson Education Ltd

Every effort has been made to trace the copyright holders and we apologise in advance for any unintentional omissions. We would be pleased to insert the appropriate acknowledgment in any subsequent edition of this publication.

Illustration Acknowledgements
Moreno Chiacchiera (Beehive Illustration), Joelle Dreidemy (Bright Agency), HL Studios, Sue King (Plum Pudding Illustration), Katie McDee, Bill McGuire (Shannon Associates), Jackie Stafford

Unit 1
My birthday

Unit 2
At school

Unit 3
Occupations

Unit 4
My body

Unit 5
Opposites

Unit 6
My house

Unit 7
Food (1)

Unit 8
Feelings